The Play of Life

THE PLAY OF LIFE

In Seven Acts

"All the world is a stage,
And all the men and women merely players;
They have their exits and their entrances;
And one man in his time plays many parts,
His acts being seven ages."
         —*Shakespeare: "As You Like It."*

BY

ALTA FLORENCE ARMSTRONG

ARTI et VERITATI

BOSTON
THE GORHAM PRESS
MCMXVII

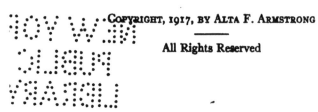

The Gorham Press, Boston, U.S.A.

TO
MY MOTHER

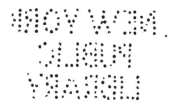

"Behold the child, by Nature's kindly law,
Pleased with a rattle, tickled with a straw;
Some livelier plaything gives his youth delight.
A little louder, but as empty quite;
Scarfs, garters, gold, amuse his riper stage,
And beads and prayer-books are the toys of age;
Pleased with this bauble still, as that before;
Till tired he sleeps, and life's poor play is o'er."

               —*"An Essay on Man"*—POPE.

PROEM

THE WORLD, A STAGE: MAN, THE ACTOR.

In the beginning, the Omnipotent gave the wonderful, interesting, beautiful WORLD as a magical stage for the Play of "Life" to be acted.

Later, he gave MAN, the Actor in the Play of "Life": Even as you,—even as every Man has been given to act his part.

Seven distinct Age Acts there are in the complete Play of "Life." No complete "Life" drama has less. No Play of "Life" has more. All of Life's Ages are in them.

It has never mattered, and it will never matter, when Man lived, where he lived, what color, who he was, or what he did: These Seven Ages are acted out in a full drama of "Life"—always, on the same old, broad, wonderful stage of the WORLD,—in the days that were, in our days,— in the days that are to be!

And so you act your part, and I act mine: You in your way, I in mine,—even as ancient man acted his part, future man will act his part,—always: "His acts being seven Ages."

"One generation passeth away, and another generation cometh: but the earth abideth forever."
—Eccl., i:4.

"All the world's a stage,
And all the men and women merely players:
They have their exits and their entrances;
And one man in his time plays many parts,
His acts being seven ages. At first the infant,
Mewing and puking in the nurse's arms.
And then the whining school-boy, with his satchel
And shining morning face, creeping like snail
Unwillingly to school. And then the lover,
Sighing like furnace, with a woeful ballad
Made to his mistress' eyebrow. Then a soldier,
Full of strange oaths and bearded like the pard,
Jealous in honor, sudden and quick in quarrel,
Seeking the bubble reputation
Even at the cannon's mouth. And then the justice,
In fair round belly with good capon lined,
With eyes severe and beard of formal cut,
Full of wise saws and modern instances;
And so he plays his part. The sixth age shifts
Into the lean and slipper'd pantaloon,
With spectacles on nose and pouch on side,
His youthful hose, well saved, a world too wide
For his shrunk shank; and his big manly voice,
Turning again toward childish treble, pipes
And whistles in his sound. Last scene of all,
That ends this strange eventful history,
Is second childishness and mere oblivion,
Sans teeth, sans eyes, sans taste, sans everything."
                —Shakespeare: "As You Like It."

"I am the vine, ye are the branches."
                —John, 15: 5.

"ALL THE WORLD'S A STAGE"

"And all the men and women merely players:
They have their exits and their entrances;
And one man in his time plays many parts,
His acts being seven ages."

THE STAR OF LIFE'S PLAY.

First Age: *"The infant,*
Mewing and puking in the nurse's arms."

Second Age:
"The whining school-boy, with his satchel
And shining morning face, creeping like snail
Unwillingly to school."

Third Age: *"The lover,*
Sighing like furnace, with a woeful ballad
Made to his mistress' eyebrow."

Fourth Age: *"A soldier,*
Full of strange oaths and bearded like the pard,
Jealous in honor, sudden and quick in quarrel,
Seeking the bubble reputation
Even at the cannon's mouth."

Fifth Age: *"The justice,*
In fair round belly with good capon lined,
With eyes severe and beard of formal cut,
Full of wise saws and modern instances."

Sixth   *"Age shifts*
Into the lean and slipper'd pantaloon,
With spectacles on nose and pouch on side,
His youthful hose, well saved, a world too wide
For his shrunk shank; and his big manly voice,
Turning again toward childish treble, pipes
And whistles in his sound."

Last Age of all:
"That ends this strange eventful history,
Is second childishness and mere oblivion,
Sans teeth, sans eyes, sans taste, sans everything."

THE PLAY OF LIFE

PROGRAMME

TIME: Past, Present, Future.

PLACE: The Stage of the World.

CAST: The Nazarene: Star of "Life."
Man: The Actor.

MANAGER: The Omnipotent.

"For me kind nature wakes her genial power,
Suckles each herb, and spreads out every flower;
Annual for me, the grape, the rose, renew
The juice nectareous and the balmy dew;
For me, the mine a thousand treasures brings;
For me, health gushes from a thousand springs;
Seas roll to waft me, suns to light me rise;
My footstool earth, my canopy the skies."
       —Pope: "Essay on Man."

"I am the way, and the truth, and the life: no man
cometh unto the Father, but by me."—John, 14: 6.

THE PLAY OF LIFE

"All the world's a stage"
—Shakespeare: "As You Like It."

The World as a Stage invites, fascinates, inspires Man to Life's activities.

The World, so wondrous in its mystic grandeur, its beauty, its loveliness, its marvelous ensemble of nature, its myriad forms of life, its extravagant scenic wonder, furnishes innumerably fashioned stage settings for Man's wonderful, *individual* Play of "Life."

The whimsical and fantastic mood of Dame Nature, when she moulded, folded, grooved, watered, painted, perfumed, lighted and shadowed this gorgeous region for Man's play-ground, truly appeased all desires of Man. The Omnipotent, in his wondrous generosity, made the Stage—yours and mine, an Annex to Heaven!

The arena for "Life's" panorama is from the East to the West; the North to the South, even in the aeronautic realm above and in the deep, dark caverns of the earth, while a few play their part on the pearly, coral bed of the ocean deep. 'Tis a Hippodrome for untiring, advancing, adventurous Man; a

13

setting for every actor, whatsoever his individual inclination may be.

To adequately convey the least conception of the sumptuousness of the maze of splendor, Nature, in her lavish mood, poured out of her cornucopia of inexhaustible beauties on this broad stage, "it would require a quill pen from one of the most gorgeous hued birds that ever lived, dipped in a fluid of concentrated mixture of a thousand selected rainbows," dissolved in millions of variegated smiling blossoms, delicately tinted by hundreds of exquisitely colored sunsets: All this—and more, to give the slightest pen analysis of the bountiful floriculture array that drapes the globe in royal garment.

Taking a panoramic view, we find spreading over the center of the World Stage that unfolds before man, a carpet of velvety emerald, shadowed and color-toned by the everchanging season's thermometer. This green expanse, figured in varied vegetation designs, as unexpected and numerous as the grain of veneer wood, suffice to excite constant admiration and anticipation. This tropical carpet of huge dimension, spreading out as plain, rolling hills and rumpled mountains, has promiscuous lake-rugs of crystal clearness that mirror their borders of multi-colored mosses and flowers, as if to send forth to our heavenly neighbors a reflected picture of our *Setting* Sublime! Spreading sheets of shimmering sand, here and there on the broad World Stage carpet, shine in jewel radiance like the blazing Sahara Solitâire that sparkles on the earth's equatorial ring.

14

This highly colored carpet is bordered by the wrinkled, misty ocean of generous spreading expanse. Its creeping fringe of waves interweave into the green expanse, making one immense world-rug. By art's supreme touch this rug is fitly finished on either end by a beautiful, broad, snow-white fringe,—and these ice-fringe threads that trail to the extreme limit of the platform, north and south, are made paths by Man!

The roof rising high above Man's stage is an immeasurable vault of mystery, forming architecture's perfect dome, kaleidoscopic in splendor,—from blustering dark storm clouds to the prismatic display of sunset's daintiest tints. It is an arched roof draped in festoons of velvet clouds; studded by millions of twinkling incandescent lights, that peep at Man through waving banners of mist,—with the Solar luminary swinging across the arch,—a chandelier of radiance.

> *"How beautiful is earth! my starry thoughts*
> *Look down on it from their unearthly sphere,*
> *And sing symphonious—Beautiful is earth!*
> *The lights and shadows of her myriad hills:*
> *The branching greenness of her myriad woods;*
> *Her sky-affecting rocks; her zoning sea;*
> *Her rushing, gleaming cataracts; her streams*
> *That race below, the winged clouds on high;*
> *Her pleasantness of vale and meadow!"*
> —*Mrs. Browning.*

With such an array of Glory above Man, of which one glimpse at the sublime envoys of nature's beauty should be sufficient to inspire him to aspire to Life's highest activities, it seems impossible to favor him, in his brief visit, with more,—yet, the bowl of beauty is made to run over, when on festival occasions a brilliant rainbow is ushered out: an *arched window into Paradise*. And to each Man, the veil back of the *"Rainbow Arch"* will rise,—the final curtain.

"And all the men and women merely players;
They have their exits and their entrances;
And one man in his time plays many parts,
His acts being seven ages."
            —*Shakespeare: "As You Like It."*

Man, the Actor.

How wonderful is he, to be so bountifully favored with such sublime Stage Settings!

Consider the minute, accurate perfection of the multifarious variety of *Stage* detail; the unobstructed course of the light beam in its years and years and years of travel, the countless complex mineralogical formations, the aroma of every flower, the flavor of fruit, the music of nature, the moulding of the icicle, the freshness of the dew-drop.

Let imagination roam back, back ages upon ages, and dwell on the millions and millions of years that gave the "Nebular Hypothesis" to decorate the roof of Man's Stage in a fiery mist of mystery; the centuries upon centuries involved in unfolding the Omnipotent's wonderful laws; the myriad years of developing geology, in preparing the incomprehensible grandeur and perfection vested in the Stage of the World, to serve, only, as a back-ground for *Man,* —the perfect fruit of God's evolution; the highest conception of God on earth!

17

> *"Flower in the crannied wall,*
> *I pluck you out of the crannies;—*
> *Hold you here, root and all, in my hand,*
> *Little flower—but if I could understand*
> *What you are, root and all, and all in all,*
> *I should know what God and Man is."*
> *—Tennyson.*

Look further, and ponder on Man's capability of wondrous thought that leaps out into the immeasurable, mysterious realms that surround him; the serene communion that is perpetual within him,— a seething of far-reaching ideas,—comprehensive, practical and reverential, mathematically proving his every thought and act! *Man,* who thrills with the emotions of joy; who is depressed by fear and grief; who radiates love,—all governed by his individual will!

We may then justly wonder at the incredible marvel of *Man,* however low his state, for through the veil of mystery that floats around evolution's "Missing Link" may be seen the divine ember that is lit in *Man* by the eternal fires.

> *"God keeps his holy mysteries*
> *Just on the outside of man's dreams;*
> *In diapason slow, we think*
> *To hear their pinions rise and sink,*
> *While they float pure beneath his eyes.*
> *Like swans adown a stream."*
> *—Mrs. Browning: "Human Life's Mystery."*

Man thus enters on the *Stage* at his given time, to play his rôle in "Life," accepting the precariousness of his stay to participate in the "Seven Ages."

18

"Through the ages one increasing purpose runs,
And the thoughts of men are widened with the process
of the suns."
—*Tennyson.*

He realizes, that whether he makes his début early
or late in the lengthy play, that his part is impor-
tant; that of all the actors who preceded, or will
follow, he is identified in the caste as the only *Man*
to act the part assigned him by the Omnipotent
Manager; that there never was, nor never will be,
another Man exactly like him, for he is a link in
the chain of the caste of men in "Life"!

> *"O dear Spirit half-lost*
> *In thine own shadow and this fleshly sign*
> *That thou art thou—who waitest being born*
> *And banish'd into mystery, and the pain*
> *Of this divisible-indivisible world*
> *Among the numerable-innumerable*
> *Sun, sun, and sun, thro' finite-infinite space*
> *In finite-infinite time—our mortal veil*
> *And shatter'd phantom of that infinite One,*
> *Who made thee unconceivably thyself*
> *Out of His whole World-self and all in all—*
> *Live thou, and of the grain and husk, the grape*
> *And ivyberry, choose; and still depart*
> *From death to death thro' life and life, and find*
> *Nearer and ever nearer Him who wrought*
> *Not Matter, nor the finite-infinite*
> *But this main miracle, that thou art thou,*
> *With power on thine own act and on the world."*
> —*Tennyson.*

Intellectual, rational and mortal *man*, a phe-
nomenon of mind and matter, with his inexplicable

19

language, sleep, emotions, dreams, conscience, sex, we cannot analyze: rather, we tell what Man *does* than what he *is*. Libraries are full of historical records of the activities of man, playing his part, in his time, since the rising of "Life's" curtain. Each Man, in his turn, appearing in the consecutive Age Scenes, governed by the same rule of development. Each man a link in the woven mesh of "Life," striving ever to play his assigned rôle efficiently, and thus contribute his part to the climax of the Play of "Life": To *Live, Love* and *Hope!*

Man, who has leaped thus far, may then ponder on his realm—back of the *"Rainbow Arch"!*

> *"The Power that hands the Rainbow in the sky—*
> *Pledge of his constant care—*
> *Dost paint the beauty of the Crimson dye;*
> *He hides thy treasures there."*

20

THE STAR OF "LIFE"

The Nazarene

Of all the stars in earth's constellation
Or shine in glorious wide arch of heav'n,
'Tis He, who on the lost earth stage Life's realm
Entered, the Star Divine at Bethlehem;
The *Nazarene,* who, in God's brief full time
Entered into Life's every Age and clime,
Encompassing all rôles of Life on earth
Giving quintessential grace to Life's worth.
For the infant found on Life's lonely stage
We have the New Bethlehem Manger Babe;
For the boy in his eager search for truth,
There is the wisdom revealed in Christ's youth.
The Actor in Life's bright garden of love
Is o'ershadowed by His Grace from above:
Christ in battle for Man's eternal Life
Set the world standard for upholding right,
And the justice of His power divine
Has been Man's Life long task just to define.
Shorn by toil, physical strength may decline
Still with hope to complete Life's divine plan,
Age is cherished, Life is panegyrized
Till the rising curtain to Paradise.
Not a throb of Man's Life but Christ the King
Rules in all Life's problems on earth supreme;

Be they inwove in places high or low,
Christ the Star Illuminative may go
And plant hope and faith in tired human hearts
And lead them up to higher thoughts and lives.
All salient aspects of human Man,
Whatever be his time, place or race clan,
May turn to the *Nazarene* Star for light,
E'en far ignorant Man errs in the night.
The perfect, spotless, sinless Star of "Life"
Bore in Gethsemane Life's sorrow strife,
And entered Death's dark gloom at Calvary
To give Man the hope resurrection ray
Of infinite truth of Man's salvation,
For eternal Life's emancipation.
                              —Alta Florence Armstrong.

*"When the fullness of the time came, God sent forth
His Son, born of woman, born under the law,*
   *That He might redeem them that were under the law,
that we might receive the adoption of sons."*
                              —Galatians, 4: 4-5.

SCENE I

FIRST AGE

"The infant,
Mewing and puking in the nurse's arms."
—Shakespeare: "As You Like It."

PROGRAMME

TIME: Past, Present, Future.
CAST: "The Infant."
SCENE: Fairyland on the World Stage.
LIGHTING: Radiance of Dawn.
ORCHESTRA: (Heard in the distance.)
    Choral by Angels.
    Gentle Zephyrs hum; Birds sing.
STAGE SUPERVISOR: The Nurse (Mother).
MANAGER: The Omnipotent.

Supporting the "Star of Life"

The Nazarene

SCENE I

FIRST AGE

"The infant,
Mewing and puking in the nurse's arms."
—Shakespeare: "As You Like It."

All is dark.

At the peep of morn, just before the veil of night is lifted, distant melodies float in across the *stage,* yet heavily shadowed, as if shrouded in a blanket of darkness,—submissive to the entrance of its superior—*Man.* Presently, in unison with a silver throated chorus far away, a shaft of delicate golden light penetrates the dark veil as a beacon of announcement to the waiting stage! Then, while Angels bombard the stage with golden arrows, tipped with dew-drop jewels, the lips of Morn, in bird chanted song, seem happy to send in with the drifting zephyrs, to the staid, sleeping old World, a serenade of flute notes, full of freshness, glory and might, while, in the Eastern wing of the stage, the Angels engage in meditation over the gift that is to be made for a season to the World.

So, with the musical message and light that flashes forth in veiled solemnity, we discover our Hero, —a dainty, dimpled, diminutive pearl of purity,

25

ushered by God's Angels on the Stage of the World, which is at once glorified by the presence of *Man, the Spark of Divinity.* In all the grand old World the nearest to God is this tiny actor; in him "Life," in all its purity and truth is vested.

As if to rival Heaven's glory, whence the infant came, the World-Stage takes on an atmosphere of exquisite delicacy and envelops the Dreamer in a fairyland of dainty elegance,—a miniature perfection that charms. Yet, while he is haunted by a delicate revelry of fancy-lore's fancifulness, and tiny elves fan him with the beams of dawn, the little visitor smiles over some secret the Angels must have whispered to him: a *secret* that has never been told! Have the Angels told him he possesses the estimable quality of winning the glories of "Life" in an humble, resigned way, or have they revealed that his *"Spark of Divinity"* will ignite the world in a fire that will blaze on the history pages of the drama of "Life"? Does he smile serenely over the knowledge that he is to be a "King Cheops," and play his part building Pyramids to awe Man; or possibly the "Emperor Ming," and contribute to "Life's" drama by founding a Dynasty? Yet, it may be he is anticipating the rôle of an "Alexander the Great," a "Shakespeare," a "Gladstone," a "Washington,"—aye, the infant dreamer may be any of these, and more, playing his part in the "First Age,"—for they all flash the Secret Smile!

"Nobody weighed the baby's smile,
Or the love that came with the helpless one. . . ."

. . . . .

26

"No index tells the mighty worth
Of little baby's quiet breath,
A soft, unceasing metronome,
Patient and faithful unto death.

Nobody weighed the baby's soul,
For here on earth no weight may be
That could avail; God only knows
Its value in eternity."
—Mrs. E. L. Beers.

Is he encouraged by this intuition to take a peep at his stage? He does so, and alas, the little actor suffers from an acute case of "stage fright." With most plaintive notes he plays on the emotions of Man. The tiny physical bundle that wraps his *Spark of Divinity* seems conscious of its utter helplessness, and touches at once the heart of the strong by his tender appeal, made in the most sorrowful notes on the harp of pathos. The cry of a babe, in its weakness, its sincerity, its lonesomeness, —not yet attune to the vibrant waves of "Life," touches the heart strings of the earth's most hardened and calloused Man,—striking the lost chord therein, making it vibrate anew in sympathy for the helplessness of the infant that is launched on the stage of "Life": The infant, who, without the care and love of Man, would perish. So, enthroned:

"Mewing and puking in the nurse's arms,"
—Shakespeare.

he is saturated with the incense of *love,* the supremest gift that floated in from Heaven,—the saving grace of Man. By this stimulating gift, the least, the strangest, is soon encouraged to trust. By the "nurse's" generous outpouring of this strengthening tonic of "Life,"—*Love,* spectrumatized in kindness, patience and generosity—the little actor is encouraged, and gradually emerges from the land of dreams to demonstrate, feebly, his desire to be identified with Man, following precisely the pattern of development his predecessors used, prompted by the spontaneity of *being.*

The infant, the dearest and newest of all "Life's" caste, is yet too much aloof from Man's tenacious exertion, spent in playing his advanced rôles in "Life," to be at once recognized as an active participant in the tense drama that is going on. He is the delicate bud of folded petals of *Mind, Heart* and *Will;* the bud of Man, that must be bathed in the sunshine of *Love,* that petal by petal he may unfold and develop into World's crowning flower!

Gradually, he is coached in the elementary cues of "Life," his "First Age" developing into a series of feature acts.

Having been convinced by Nature's intuition that he *IS;* experimentally, he timidly tests, one by one, his presentative powers. How he blinks and squints with those first peeps, as if coquetting with sight. The little curtains rise and fall that he may retreat, intermittently, into the "Land of Dreams," until he becomes accustomed to his surroundings. Yet, while he is privileged recesses from the sensation of sight, secretly, unconsciously, he records on the clean slate of his mind the waves of sound that beat on his miniature organ, varying up and down the scale, from the pelting, unharmonious waves of an earth's tempestuous storm, to a mother's soothing song. The current of contact develops wonderful confidence in the new actor: the magnetic current of touch seems the satisfying link to humanity. How delicately, yet with all his strength, he cleaves to anything that passes his way. A weak grasp on the world, but who can tell how strong that "grasp on the world" may ultimately become!

The flavors of life that tickle his senses of taste and smell are introduced so gradually, and with possibly less force, that he is less demonstrative in their recognition. We, however, enjoy his evident relish of his "Milk of Life," and observe his keen detection of substances of foreign flavor.

From constant exercise of his discovered senses, we notice his representative power feebly develop. He recognizes a touch: the fondling of his Nurse at once contents him; her voice is soon discriminated from other sounds that float in on his tiny drum. He associates the touch and the voice, then he witnesses its source by seeing. Gradually, these powers are registered in faintest imprint in the index of his intellect; at first, not for what they are, but as essential elements for "Life's" intellectual cues.

Spontaneously, as physical strength is poured into his little body, he toys with these interesting attributes of "Life," exercising them madly in one round of confusion. Every color entrances him, every movement invites him to ecstasy, every sound attracts, and in response his movements are jumbled.

He wiggles and kicks in all directions. These reflective flashes of observation prove the appendant of knowledge in Man.

This intellectual petal of the bud of Man is the first that attracts us by unfolding; then curls back, slightly, the petal of the *Heart,* the sensibilities. Buoyed by the intoxicating spirit of existence, he begins to vibrate with emotions, and bubbles forth from the delicate temple that encases him joyously cooing, gurgling in laughter and exploding in tears. These waves of emotion that play over him find expression in unregulated bouncing and flouncing.

Then the development of physical control is quite noticeable. He discovers his extravagance in movements, and uses reserve, confining his movements to those that prove sufficient for the occasion. Attracted by an alluring object, we see him reach for it with definite aim; so, by repetition of this satisfying experience, his fluttering movements are subjected to a precise orderly coördination.

We see him venture totteringly, fearlessly forth on the path of "Life," giving his exhaustless interest, absorbingly to the matter-of-fact settings that border his entrance. Vivid, penetrating impressions are made on his delicate mind by his first contacts with the World's wonderful offerings for instruments in working out "Life's" plot. How he accepts unhesitatingly as his (as the Omnipotent intended Man always to do), the beautiful flower by the way, the shining pebble in the path, or the equally wonderful inorganic substance of a clod of dirt;—all, to the trustful, fearless child being equally attractive, until he has them familiarized and definitely catalogued. His initial contacts with important essential objects—the home, the horse, the dog, the machine—stand out impressively by their marvelous significance, only to be, by repetition, indelible facts that link the actor to the Stage of the World. Thus, he darts restlessly here and there in eager pursuance of the bewildering stage furnishings,—learning their names and uses in supporting and promoting his activities.

How the playthings of "Life" attract him! A stick, a ball, a pool of water, bewitch him, while a wiggling fish, a flying bird, a grazing horse, charm him. We witness him in ecstasy over the quivering movements of a singing bird that pours forth floods of delirious music; pensive as he visits the pelting waves that roll in on the sunny, sandy seashore, innocently dissolving all mystery. The moon and the stars furnish an animation of study. The blink of his trustful, appreciative, observing eye seems the only true understanding of the magnanimous! He proves himself a scientist in the truest sense by the startling rapidity of his comprehension and definite indexing of the World's innumerable *settings*. So, the untiring, undoubting investigator, prompted ever by his instinct for adventure, pushes persistently on into "Life's" buzzing, humming, widening field.

The infant, who thus expands in the simple luxury of *being* in the first hours of "Life's" morning, is not exaggeratedly prolonged, for from exercise of the higher faculties the young actor consciously

31

formulates his knowledge and soon develops a comprehensive understanding that "Life is real, Life is earnest," which sinks deep in his fancy free, untarnished soul, where inconceivable secretive emotions soliloquize and confidences seethe, making him a *child*.

This fresh, unencumbered, non-resisting child proves the most fertile soil for mental growth in the garden of "Life." The harvest from his uncultivated mind, with but an oasis of wisdom, is, with a little irrigation, bountiful in the fruits of simple abstractions, clear reasoning about concrete things, mastered and comprehensive languages, mathematical estimates, the understanding of social laws and the ethics of his day. The ease with which he masters and comprehends "Life's" cues, during the successive *child* years; his display of perfect logic and mature faculties astound the adult observer. His precocity for "Life's" essential knowledge about his Stage of the World, in certain ways, is equal to that of any later Age, for during the few brief years of his childhood his physical and mental foundations are substantially constructed of the common, matter-of-fact stones, all cemented in perfect symmetry, with the mortar of experience, with all the skill of an accomplished mason of knowledge. On this foundation he constructs the complete framework for "Life's" building, which he sheaths and decorates during his following Ages, as the *"Man"* architect indulges his will.

32

SCENE II

SECOND AGE

*"The whining school-boy, with his satchel
And shining morning face, creeping like snail
Unwillingly to school."*
—Shakespeare: "As You Like It."

PROGRAMME

TIME: Past, Present, Future.
CAST: "The whining school-boy."
SCENE: The World in miniature.
LIGHTING: First clear rays of Morning.
ORCHESTRA: Selections from "Nature."
STAGE SUPERVISORS: Coaches.
MANAGER: The Omnipotent.

Supporting the "Star of Life"

The Nazarene

SCENE II

SECOND AGE

"The whining school-boy, with his satchel
And shining morning face, creeping like snail
Unwillingly to school."
—*Shakespeare: "As You Like It."*

A gentle, sympathetic harmony peacefully throbs from Nature's varying symphony; a piping solo of a bird's cheery morning greeting; a sonata from the tuneful breezes and vibrating leaves; an orchestration of sorrowful lamentations of Nature's wailing winds and melancholy waves, gathering, swelling and soaring to the frenzied anguish of a tempestuous hurricane! Then, sinking, gradually, to the gentle rhythmical patter of a crystal rain shower,—penetrated by a far-off gleam of morning's crimson banners, to light the wavering path of:

"The whining school-boy, with his satchel
And shining morning face, creeping like snail
Unwillingly to school."
—*Shakespeare.*

Thus, we are greeted by the Actor that graces the "Second Age,"—the veriest mystery that appears under the curved theatrical dome, he, the heir to "Life"!

35

With his worldly estate and cues to his activities fairly well charted, we see him, in a perfectly sure and familiar manner, venture leisurely forth to survey the "How and the Why" of the allotment "Life" holds for him:

"Why two and two make four? Why round is not
    square?
Why the rock stands still, and the light clouds fly?
Why the heavy oak groans, and the white willows sigh?
Why deep is not high, and high is not deep?"
                        —Tennyson.

—to be, during this excursion of inspection, a blessing, a trouble, a rest, a burden, a torment,—and yet the bubbling joy of "Life's" Play that is in full swing. Life's song would lose its charm without the mischief, wit and glee of the carefree, indolent, ever idle, always busy boy.

He seems far more interested in the Stage properties than the theme of "Life," and in this indifferent, self-confident, unpretentious state, we have an actor truly natural. Artificial activity is foreign to him. He acts independently, catering not to applause of Coach, Audience or Manager, but willingly loses himself among the by-ways of Nature, as her reverent student.

The glow of curiosity seems continued from his "First e" to anchor him securely in his "Second Scene." He instinctively feels himself kin to all life, organic and inorganic, and hungeringly grasps all unvarnished truths,—those that are not enameled by the sham of "Life." Thus, he recedes to the

36

shadow and shelter of Nature to be an integral part, intensely interested in all that is "awfully vast and elegantly little"; learning the habits and ways of the plants in the World's garden, that saturate the atmosphere with their sweet, penetrating perfumes, their ever-varying dress; studying the system of the waters, their rise and fall, their ebb and flow in the nervous throb of "Life"; makes acquaintances and comrades with the animals of the woods; examines the mineralogical and horticultural formations of the earth; meditates over the fleeting meteors of the sky,—so closely associating himself with these inanimate substances that he steals Nature's heart and penetrates the mysteries over which his scientific elders deliberate. So harmoniously is he blended with Nature that he grows freely with the young plants, busying himself with a hundred nothings; beginning many things, finishing none; forgetting on the morrow the plans of the previous day; a term of idleness, a term of revery,—the primitive state of a savage, without his labors, without his anxiety,— lost, repeatedly, in soliloquy over Nature's workings, possibly the going and coming of an insect, the caprices of a beetle; indolent, yet busy, without object, but leading, nevertheless, indirectly, to a thought, and,

> *"The thoughts of Youth are long, long thoughts."*
> —*Longfellow.*

In the Springtime of "Life," the seed planting season, seeds of *Truth* are imbedded in the broad,

37

fertile, untilled field of the boy's mind by *direct* and *indirect* sowing. Multitudinous seeds, like those of the earth, each having a peculiarity of form and purpose, which, after being imbedded in the mind and nourished with time, blossom forth in "Life's" harvest time in myriad forms.

Like the vegetable species, seeds planted in different soils and climates propagate in proportion to the quality of the soil and zone, some developing into perfection, others shriveling to death; seeds similar in appearance, yet the off-springs are so different,—from the fairest flowers to great sturdy oaks. So it is in planting the seeds of *Truth* in the boy's mind; some may take deep root and grow, others struggle along, possibly die. Some *Truth* may cause him to blossom into a beautiful poet, rising to general and transcendental truths, while other truths may make him a strong, sturdy pine in the forest of Men, swaying not with the winds of sin.

The boy, with his wild strange ways, his queer remarks and odd replies, sometimes foolish, often wise, is now invited to the *directed* planting of the tiny seeds, which contain within them the root of "Life." The Stage Supervisors of this Age are now linked with his activities, as he is coached in "Life's" truths that have aided his predecessors. His field of mind is plowed, harrowed, and in definite direct lines, the seeds are planted, nurtured and cultivated by whatever instruments and tools peculiar to his time and place, so that at the harvest season there will be no barren places, no weeds, but straight accessible rows of ripened fruit, easily harvested.

38

Eagerly he accepts from "Life's" older participants the threads of knowledge that serve in the toils, problems and needs of "Life," that are unraveled for him by diverse ways, tutored according to the peculiar custom of his day, whether in an edifice of knowledge that offers an assimilated, classified routine of development, where he is coached by blackboard, globe, map or book; or he enjoys this blissful scene by letting experience suffice as Coach. Nevertheless, in either event, aided or unaided, this term of learning *about* things, this absorbing state of being, throws a glow around the lad, —an aureole that emphatically distinguishes this period from others so closely associated, yet so foreign.

He soon feels burdened with his conception of things as they are, and in the conceit of his perception of the practical assets of "Life" (for he feels that he knows all worth knowing), with yet no hint as to his later wonderful participation in the Battle of "Life," his thirst of curiosity seems temporarily quenched, which causes the glow it supported to vanish. So, self-confident in his beautiful ignorance, he indulges in an adolescent recess in the Springtime of "Life," without glow, care or doubt,—deliberately "w a i t i n g," a dormant volcanic Man! The lad, small and unpretentious, neither receding nor proceeding, is s t i l l, like the surface of a quiet lake, high on a pinnacle of a mountain, sheltered from the winds by a giant granite wing: a lake so small an elk might leap across; so still, its mirrored surface, by transparency deception, invites exploration of its smooth, sandy, apparently shallow bed, yet to one probing the depth of such an unpretentious, tiny, quiet pool, unfathomable depths are revealed which plumbing line cannot reach! So it is with the boy, enjoying the placid years of adolescence, without revealing a ripple of the wave of enthusiasm, apparently spiritually asleep, shallow, crude, earthy,—yet, the depth of a boy's soul cannot be fathomed! The latent powers, physically, intellectually and spiritually, that might be unearthed from the unattractive, coarse, ruggedness beneath the quiet surface of the boy, by the pressure of time and friction of battle, may be wrought the finest gems of the world. There may be in the calm, secluded lake of the boy's soul, buried treasures that he will dig out, refine and polish and offer them as a gift to the world; possibly in the form of a voice that will thrill the Stage of "Life" with ecstasy, judicial power that will enable him to wield the scepter over man,—some richness that will glisten in its pureness and hold the record for art's perfection.

Thus, the boy's stream of "Life" flows gently on from this quiet lake, flowing over the rock-ribbed mountain-side, eroding and adjusting its path to the least resistance and in the sweeping progress of the flow, particle by particle, all in the same direction, growing in size and strength, his "Life" develops into a peaceful, well-directed stream of pronounced current to press on the lock of youth, which, when unlocked, results in a torrent of force in the current of the stream of "Life."

SCENE III

THIRD AGE

"The lover,
Sighing like furnace, with a woeful ballad
Made to his mistress' eyebrow."
—Shakespeare: "As You Like It."

PROGRAMME

TIME: Past, Present, Future.
CAST: "The Lover."
SCENE: Valley of Dreamland.
LIGHTING: Splashed in Shimmering Sunshine.
ORCHESTRA: Song on the chords of the Heart.
STAGE SUPERVISOR: Love's Mistress.
MANAGER: The Omnipotent.

Supporting the "Star of Life"

The Nazarene

41

SCENE III

THIRD AGE

"The lover,
Sighing like furnace, with a woeful ballad
Made to his mistress' eyebrow."
—Shakespeare: "As You Like It."

"All the world loves a lover," so with what eagerness we anticipate the entrance of the actor who is to play this fascinating rôle. The curtain scarcely lowers on the boy enjoying his recess of "Life," until it rises again, and, as the caterpillar is transformed into a brilliant-hued butterfly, so the dull, quiescent actor of the closing act of the "Second Scene" appears before us clothed in the beautiful airy wings of *Youth,* the "Lover" of "Life,"

"With a dream 'neath his waking eyelids hidden
And a frequent sigh unbidden."
—Mrs. Browning.

The song of his awakened heart is the tuning fork by which the melody of "Life" is keyed.

"Quick with youth's strong, sweet story,—thirsting now to play the *Man,"*—his thrilling interpretation of the song of his Heart instantaneously portrays the perfection of his being. As the petals of

43

the flower open out to drink in the rich rays of the sun's radiance and pour out in return its rare fragrance and adorn by its perfection, so *Youth,* the brightest flower of the world, basking in the sunshine of "Life," unfolds before us in this act his beautiful petals of *Mind, Heart* and *Will* to full-blown blossom.

In sympathetic response we follow him, as he advances, buoyantly, on the stage, which is for a second time. a "Fairyland on the World Stage,"—a Valley of Dreamland, dotted by fountains of Hope, studded by springs of Purity, threaded by streams pressed with currents of Energy, strengthened by glaciers of Courage,—a Valley where the realities of "Life's" difficult tasks roll off into indistinct mountains, hazy on the distant horizon, framing the dazzling picture of *Youth's* Dreamland!

To *Youth,* possessing the temperament in the June of Life, the *stage* is perennially gay; he bubbles over with the enlivening spirit of happiness, Youth's chief ornament;

"Happy, not in what it has, but in what it is:
Not in possessing much, but in hoping and loving much."

Indifferent things are pleasant to him, sad things are soon driven out of his mind, care and misfortune rest easily upon him,—he lives in the future, building for the climax of "Life," and this hope, this anticipation, paint everything for him in their gorgeous colors, hiding the displeasing things of "Life."

The actor of Scene III, having drunk from the cup of "Life" during the placid ages, is now intoxicated with it, and we see surging upon him the inevitable tide of Youth's bubbling activities to follow the pattern of tradition. Like the waves of the ocean's indefatigable tides, pressing and breaking in shattered sprays, filling full every channel and arm of the sea, so the spirit of *Youth* comes gleaming and roaring irresistibly on the shore of time, gradually advancing, filling and overflowing all our actor's channels of "Life" with Love, Faith and Hope.

From the splashing onrush of the tide of *Youth,* we see the frothy foam thereof wafted helter-skelter, but the essential strength is anchored in the stirring of the deep waters of Life, the turbulent power of enthusiasm, the backbone of effort, making " 'Youth' another way to spell 'Life.' " During this age of "Life," man makes of himself a storage battery of enthusiasm, love, courage, faith, religion,—the virtues of "Life," that support him for the remainder of his time; his future activity depending virtually on the strength of his battery of *Youth,* for Youth is concentrated life.

This stimulating tide of enthusiasm that rises in *Youth* brings to the surface many different elements, traits and emotions that lend at once a flourish to his acting, riveting our attention. We are held spellbound by his extravagant expenditure of life's vitalities. The unruly whirlpools of rationalism, melancholy and gay moods, inchoation, impulsiveness, venturesomeness and radicalism, each in themselves danger signals and sink holes, awe us with fear for our actor's safety until they are sucked in

45

by the strong current of "Life" that is pushed on by the force of *knowledge* of "Life," *love* of "Life" and *will* to live, which harmoniously blend the actor's widely varying tendencies into a directed power on its endless course, daringly competitive in its inexhaustible strength.

The actor of this age of untranslatable yearnings, of confused vehement emotions, of all sorts of spiritual awakenings, with his wealth of energy spilling in whatsoever action his temperament prompts indulgence, nibbles hungrily the fruit of the tree of knowledge of Good and Evil. Eagerly, he seeks to experience the whispers of his phantasm and pursues the fancy of his *hope*.

His optimistic view of the present and glorious hopefulness for the future blossoms into the flower of love, the pure, ethereal love of life, its living;— the love of ideals, love of cause, love of art, religion, love of his fellow actors in the cast of "Life," and it is this magnanimous *love* that proves the leaven of "Life" that ferments and makes this Age rise to the highest! This illuminative truth is strikingly exemplified in the actor's sincere, fervent, unselfish love for the

"Queen of his Age." It exalts him into sanctity and in celestial mystery he bows submissively. "One pair of eyes are worshiped, one voice is all there is of music."

"The lover,
Sighing like furnace, with a woeful ballad
Made to his mistress' eyebrow.
—Shakespeare: "As You Like It."

46

We see an age robed in the warmth of love, covering all blemishes, transforming them into beauty, leveling all inequalities. This wonderful warmth of love—would that it would never cool!

With the full unfolding of the petal of the Heart, the

> *". . . . Loving thoughts that start*
> *Into being are like perfume from the*
> *blossom of the heart."*

The winds seem to blow balmier, the skies seem to wear a softer blue, the sunsets seem more gorgeous, the moonlight seems purer, the birds seem gayer, the flowers brighter, the brook's song sweeter as it dances along over its pebbly bed. This hallowing melts all "Life's" realities in sympathy with the joyous, rosy-hued realization of "Life" and its wondrous value. By this *Love,* which is the moral law of man, the actor's every gesture, every phase of "Life's" philosophy of expression, is tempered.

As at a loom, on the chains of *knowledge* and *ignorance,* the youthful actor, rich in his inheritance of "Life's" wonderful threads, experimentally starts weaving them, using some threads extravagantly, others sparingly, with no apparent definiteness of outline or uniformity of texture. With the fine silken threads of joy, hope, love, he weaves homespun yarns of grief, fear and hatred, ravelings of temptation and sin, twisted with golden strands of religion. Gradually, as the threads unwind from the shuttle of selected occupation, a pronounced pattern de-

47

velops, being governed primarily by the woof of circumstance, drawn by the tension of his *will*.

The "Life" Scene of *Youth*, which the child dreams of, is the cherished "Age" of "Life." *Youth*, the radiant Age of man, that "psychologists have scrutinized, philosophers have discoursed upon, cynics have sneered at," pessimists have fought against, artists have painted, poets have exalted in rhyme, musicians have sung about, has never been completely caught, except as we catch a glimpse of the intangible and fleeting scene as played by Man on the broad stage of "Life." This evasiveness furnishes the real charm of "Life's" supreme scene, acted in the quintessence of living beauty.

> *"The tissues of the life to be*
> *He weaves with colors all his own,*
> *And in the fields of destiny*
> *He reaps as he has sown."*

SCENE IV

FOURTH AGE

"A Soldier,
Full of strange oaths and bearded like the pard,
Jealous in honor, sudden and quick in quarrel,
Seeking the bubble reputation
Even at the cannon's mouth."
—Shakespeare: "As You Like It."

PROGRAMME

TIME: Past, Present, Future.

CAST: "The Soldier."

SCENE: Battlefield of "Life."

LIGHTING: High Noon.

ORCHESTRA: March of Time.

STAGE SUPERVISORS: The World of Actors.

MANAGER: The Omnipotent.

Supporting the "Star of Life"

The Nazarene

SCENE IV

FOURTH ACT

> *"A Soldier,*
> *Full of strange oaths and bearded like the pard,*
> *Jealous in honor, sudden and quick in quarrel,*
> *Seeking the bubble reputation*
> *Even at the cannon's mouth."*
> *—Shakespeare: "As You Like It."*

Simultaneously, with the penetrating bugle call of life's need, that floats out over *Youth's* valley of tranquillity, we see the actor in the distance respond, and advance toward "Life's" Scene of Battle that lies so near. He rapidly approaches, leaving *Youth's* radiant "Dreamland" in the background, gradually dimming and fading into a luminous vapory halo circling the youthful actor. He turns and gazes back over *Youth's* playground for one fond caress of the sunshine he basked in, the rich fruits he feasted on and stored away,—sweeping the invitingly smooth lay with one lingering glance of love, which proves only to emphasize the raw, rugged, glaring, gigantic mountains of life's precariousness that jut up appallingly before him—"Life's" Battlefield, so closely hugging his beautiful valley!

Thus, on the brink of his Fourth Age, he pauses to survey the rough, jagged, treacherous, rocky mountains of tribulation, disappointment, evil, disease, catastrophes; the sharp blades and snags of "Life's" accidents, to scar, wound, deter and destroy Man walking "Life's" path. As poison is poison, possibly in differently-shaped vials, under different labels, so "Life's" adversities in all the shifting scenes of time, past and present, are the same, clothed differently.

Decision is thrust upon him. Either he is to oppose or relax, tragically waste his strength or end the battle in joyful exuberant victory. The tenseness of the hour of decision, how it thrillingly electrifies!

Over and above the stair-step mountains of Adversity he sees the soaring, invincible, immortal peak of infinite *Truth* that always prevails, whatsoever his point of view, directing, inviting Man to put on the armor for adversity and make the peerless climb. After taking in the "setting" of the Battlefield of "Life," we see him experiencing the soliloquy of "Life": "To be or not to be, that is the question." Thunderingly, dawns upon him the realization of his individual responsibility to his Manager, the *Omnipotent,* and how he has heretofore been privileged the easy, delightful, beautiful rôles of "Life," and that the perfection, exaltation and perpetuation of the "Play of Life" depend solely on the heroism of its actors in the Age of strife, service and tragedy, —the Age he now finds himself in. This overwhelming conviction induces all that is within him— the virtues that have been growing during his previous Ages—to blossom forth in unison to a con-

52

sciousness of his enormous endowment to be a crea-
ture of *Eternity* rather than of *Time,*—no longer
a parasite, but privileged an opportunity to engage
in the performance of "Life's" difficult tasks, in his
given time, *"Now,"* the narrow isthmus between
two eternities, the past and future.

> *"Full of strange oaths and bearded like the pard—"*
> *—Shakespeare.*

His quest of *Truth* determined, he enlists on the
muster roll for War against the enemies of "Life"
that tend to warp Man; to battle with Nature, men
and with himself; a War from which there is no
discharge, selecting his armor with care from the
resources of his accumulated virtues:

> *"Girdle of Truth,*
> *Brestplate of Righteousness,*
> *Shield of Faith,*
> *Sword of the Spirit,*
> *Helmet of Salvation,*
> *Feet shod with Readiness,—"*
> *—Ephesians, 6: 13-17.*

and with the ammunition of *Youth,* ignited by the
spark "Dare," the conflict of conquest is on!

His high appreciation of his newly assumed rôle in
"Life" weaves itself into a well-defined virtue of
Duty, that links the actor to his *Omnipotent* Man-
ager, stimulating his effort to play his part in fullest
veneration.

In assuming the rôle of the Soldier in "Life," he
enlists to give his life; to give back that which "Life"
has given him; physical aid to the weak, cheer to
the weary, knowledge to the dull, courage to the

53

fearing, hope to the faithless,—gives of his heart to Man and Manager, in sincere appreciation of "Life's" participation, by striving passionately to perfect and exalt his rôle,—pouring out his contribution to sustain, produce, perpetuate and perfect the plot of "Life." Whatsoever may be his rank in the army of men, whether "Private," "Lieutenant" or "General," he enters equally into the spirit of the cause, selecting from Life's armory any one of the commonly used weapons, and. by exercising confidence in his skill, may push to the front rank, a *Man* of Men. He may select a pen, like Milton, and with a drop of ink make millions think; a chisel, like Michael Angelo, and transform rugged rocks into lines of symmetrical beauty and expression; a brush, as Apelles, and with art's supreme touch deceive the beasts of the fields with a splash of paint. He may, through the strength of his enthusiastic determination kept constantly burning in a hard gem-like flame, register himself on "Life's" stage a genius,—a King of Achievement, taking his part in the battle as a "Cæsar," to rule; a "Demosthenes," an "Antony," oratorical canons, whose powerful utterances, good and bad, echo over the stage of man, age after age; a "Copernicus," who blazed the path leading to astronomy; a "Descartes," the father of philosophy; a "Confucius"; an "Isaac. Newton." Aye, he may be any one of "Life's" Generals in the varied spheres of man's activity, in any of the different countries, under their peculiar circumstances and conditions; be he a prodigy in the realm of science, philosophy, anatomy, geology, the-

54

ology, poetry, music or literature, since all of these capabilities are in him, more or less, his participation depending on his *volition* as to which one or more he may select to contribute his power in making *his* fight, in *his* battle, in *his* way, following the banner of *Truth,* as *he* sees it. Yet,

"The world knows nothing of its greatest men," —for, no less, in promoting the Manager's plan of "Life" are the faithful fathers of these wonderful men that lead in "Life's" battle; the "torch-bearers," those men that pitch the tents for shelter, shovel the fort embankment for protection, build the bridges for "Life's" army to pass over; those *great* men of no renown, who, lost in the vast number of men, as a pearl in a strand of perfect beads, one so like another, loses its identity in the circle strand, yet of itself holds a priceless premium for its intricate perfection.

> *"They have no place in storied page;*
> *No rest in marble shrine.*
> *They are past and gone with a perished age;*
> *That died and 'made no sign.'*
> *But work that shall find its wages yet,*
> *And deeds that their* Manager *will not forget,*
> *Done for their love divine—*
> . . . .
> *"Oh seek them not where sleep the dead.*
> *Ye shall not find their trace.*
> *No graven stone is at their head;*
> *No green grass hides their face.*
> *But sad and unseen is their silent grave—*
> *It may be the sand or the deep sea wave,*
> *Or a lonely desert place—*
> . . . .

"They healed sick hearts till theirs were broken,
And dried sad tears till theirs lost sight;
We shall know at last by a certain token
How they fought and fell in the fight.
Salt tears of sorrow unbeheld,
Passionate cries unchronicled,
And silent strifes for the right—
Angels shall count them and the earth shall sigh
That she left her best Actors *to battle and die."*
—Sir Edwin Arnold.

The heart of every man, first and last, is haunted by an ideal, an aspiration to *achieve* that bends all that is within him to a purpose, galvanizing him. It is the clustering of his daily deeds to a clearly defined focus that enables him to play his part to completion.

"Jealous in honor, sudden and quick in quarrel,
Seeking the bubble reputation
Even at the cannon's mouth."
—Shakespeare: "As You Like It."

The flash of vanity in him has to be satisfied. He wishes to distinguish himself in performing "Life's" tasks, whatsoever vocation he elects to follow, whether weaving a basket, digging a canal, building a house, writing a song,—according to his *idea, will* and *time* of acting. To the fulfillment of the possibilities of his manhood in the Army of "Life," he fights on, continually plodding, moment by moment, day after day, all through the Age. He persistently strains to the point of fatigue the forces within him, at the sacrifice of body and brain,—yet husbanding health, driving steadily toward *his*

56

"Mountain-Top" of *Truth*, ultimately, by fortitude and persistence, to achieve!

In this Age of distinction, it is difficult to discern any single man actor; he may be any one of many, since no two actors play their parts alike, therefore observance of any one participant would not coincide with the activities of another. Each man so different, yet all so much alike, each fighting so differently, yet all so much alike, portraying vivid contrast by their varied manifestations, for man's *will* predominates, shaping his destiny. He enacts his aspirations, his emotions, his dreams, according to his vision, acting:

> "*. . . In the living Present,*
> *Heart within, and God o'erhead!"*
> *—Longfellow.*

So, our Actor *distinguishes* himself in this Age, in a way peculiar to himself, yet his "distinction" in the fight may be *good* or *bad,* with or without *Glory.* He who links Glory with his distinction, whatsoever his rank in the army of "Life," is he who is ever mindful of performing his part in act and spirit to approach as nearly as possible to the Perfect Actor of "Life"; as the *Star of Life's Stage* would perform the same rôle, according to the actor's knowledge thereof. This battle for "distinction," which, if not all of "Life's" plot, is an all-important part of the drama. The actor's gain of "distinction," be it wisdom, wealth, culture, skill, fame or power, his laurel of *Glory* and heroism in the fight is measured by the one given standard:

his knowledge of *"The Star of Life."*

As the potter may from clay make mud or transform it into the finest china of moulded vases of rare beauty, so man, the potter of his rôle in "Life's" Fourth Scene, enjoys free volition to make "mud" of his rôle, or refine, mould and burn it in the heated strategy of battle into rare crystal beauty.

As the mysterious, tremendously valuable radium substance is contained in the very mire, so should the potter of this scene *will* to make "mud" of his rôle, by violating social, moral and natural laws, and in his low state of being, deliberately spatter "Life's" stage with his mud of injustice, greed, lust, perfidy, dishonesty, selfishness, hatred or inhumanity, we must not forget that smothered deep in his sliminess smoulders the radium *"Spark of Divinity"* to blaze up with the first inviting current that tends to draw it from the bog.

> *"No life is wasted in the great worker's hand;*
> *The gem too poor to polish in itself*
> *We grind to brighten others."*
> —*Philip James Bailey.*

"China" or "Mud," beautiful or scarred, each result will be according to the determined purpose of the potter of the rôle. Good or bad, each act of man will be as the intent of the deed, either to adorn "Life's" stage with an ornament of beauty and usefulness or smear and smudge with mud.

> *"As much eternal springs the cloudless skies,*
> *As man forever temperate, calm and wise."*

58

Yet, in "Life's" play, an accident may happen. The potter may with earnest effort and great skill mould and refine a rare and fine china ornament that, by some accident, through ignorance, becomes cracked, shattered and spoiled. So our actor's purpose, be it ever so well defined, may be broken and thrown into chaos by "Life's" accidents. The good, innocent, honest and courageous may, by ignorance, misdirection or betrayal be thrown into the lurid turmoil and become derelicts in the sea of "Life."

It is in the derelict actor that we see the sting of existence portrayed; the ignorant in his pitiful state; the scoundrel in his infamy; the pious in his jealousy; the hypocrite in his pretence; the fool in his grotesque interpretation of "Life's" plot;—"Life's" shivering, disinherited, villainous out-cast that actively weaves his hindering acts in and out, menacing "Life's" plot. Yet, this malicious character, who clings tenaciously to his villainous rôle, in the "Play of Death," is no less interesting than he who battles earnestly with the army to support "Life's" plot. In fact, the derelict's participation excites constant attention. We are alert, watching for his treachery; awed by his complete badness; pitying his ignorance; sympathizing with his foolishness; keyed to a high strain of suspicion of every act of the dynamite destroyer that plants himself on "Life's" battlefield to explode and destroy man's highest purposes.

Thus, we may see our Soldier actor in the Fourth Scene of his time, according to his individual *mind, heart* and *will*, acting his part in the Battle of

59

"Life," using whatsoever weapon that meets the
emergency of his time and place, stimulated ever
by the same spirit that lives in every soldier's heart,
weak or strong, as the case may be. Be he:

"John, Peter, Robert or Paul,
  God in his wisdom created them all;
  John a statesman, Peter a slave,
  Robert a preacher and Paul—a knave.
  Evil or good, as the case might be,
  White or colored, bond or free—
  John, Peter, Robert, and Paul,
  God in his wisdom created them all.

"Out of earth's elements, mingled with flame,
  Out of life's compounds of glory and shame,
  Fashioned and shaped by no will of their own,
  And helplessly into life's history thrown;
  Born by the law that compels man to be,
  John, Peter, Robert, and Paul,
  Born to conditions they could not foresee,
  God in his wisdom created them all.

John the head and heart of his state,
  Trusted and honored, noble and great;
  While Peter 'neath life's burdens did groan,
  .   .   .   .   .
Robert, great glory and honor received,
  .   .   .   .   .
While Paul, of the pleasures of sin took his fill,
  The purpose of Life was fulfilled in them all."
            —Anonymous.

The harsh clamor of the firing-line strife gives
the soldier a secretive zest for living. The tossing
about in the tempest battle, the problems solved,
difficulties unraveled, perplexities endured and ene-

mies conquered, toughens him. The grinding of "Life's" spears against his shield of welded virtues, the frictional rubbing of his onward battering pressure toward his purpose elect, polishes the precious gem of his manhood, making him a radiant jewel, to reflect the shining light of the Perfect Soldier,— the Hero of the Battle of "Life,"—*The Nazarene.*

SCENE V

FIFTH AGE

> *"The Justice,*
> *In fair round belly with good capon lined,*
> *With eyes severe and beard of formal cut,*
> *Full of wise saws and modern instances."*
> *—Shakespeare: "As You Like It."*

PROGRAMME

TIME: Past, Present, Future.

CAST: "The Justice."

SCENE: Mountain-top of "Life."

LIGHTING: Afternoon.

ORCHESTRA: "Victory."

STAGE SUPERVISOR: Himself.

MANAGER: The Omnipotent.

Supporting the "Star of Life"

The Nazarene

63

SCENE V

FIFTH AGE

"The Justice,
In fair round belly with good capon lined,
With eyes severe and beard of formal cut,
Full of wise saws and modern instances."
—Shakespeare: "As You Like It."

Viewing the masterful rocks and desolate cliffs
that build themselves, stanch and secure one above
another, into gigantic mountains, to soar aloof in
majestic strength, we see the scene, which in the
blazing sunlight of "Life's" Battlefield appeared
gruesome, now wonderfully softened by the shadow-
ing tints of the sun's golden rays that slip over the
Mountain-top, penetrating the grotesqueness of the
scene, painting the picture in royal shades of purple
and gold, a gorgeous array of "Victory" in har-
mony with the "Justice," who appears in the Fifth
Scene of "Life," as the acme of things accomplished,
having victoriously climbed to the apex of his rôle
in "Life." He, the heir of the Ages, stands on his
Mountain-top of "Life," in the acting of his time
and place. His time may date back to the early
swing of "Life's" rude, crude, barbaric day,—to the
dim-distant, aboriginal activity; the "Cliff Dwell-
ers" in their caves; the "Tribes"; the scenes during

65

"Life's" "Dark Ages"; the "Christian Era"; the "Mediæval Period," or he may be a character actor in the immediate weighty age, when the entire cast of actors on the stage of "Life," from the east to the west, the north to the south, through the throbbing mechanical hearts of telegraphy and telephone, are linked closer and stronger together, so that man's every act, instantaneously, as it were, penetrates through the entire system, subjecting "Life's" stage of action to be daily shaken by man's modern activity: thunderbolts of science, theology, philosophy, commerce and tragic barbaric slaughter. In whatsoever age and whatsoever place,—be it among the northern crystal bergs of ice, the swaying orange groves of the "Holy Land" or in the sleeping southlands,—anywhere; on island, continent or sea, we may find the "Justice" on his individual "Mountaintop," whether his summit be a pinnacle of the average, irregular range, or one of the high peaks that loom up sublimely.

In a semi-state of tranquillity, he watches from his station on the lofty wall the troubled sea of "Life" that flows beneath, looking afar to those Ages that have slipped away; those Scenes of "Life's" twisting and turning roads that he has stumbled over and made:

> *"Footprints on the sands of time."*
>
> *"Footprints, that perhaps another,*
> *Sailing o'er life's solemn main,*
> *A forlorn and shipwrecked brother,*
> *Seeing, shall take heart again."*
> *—Longfellow.*

66

His high, distant view of former scenes of "Infant," "Boyhood," "Youth" and "Soldier," with the gladness of their good and the sadness of their bad, now seem, through the veil of the past, other than they used to appear; good not so good; ill not so ill.

Withdrawn from "Life's" clamoring activity into the rarefied atmosphere of the azure world, he meditatively examines himself, objectively and without illusions, inquiring into the success of his elected purpose in the grand drama. He searches his encyclopedia of experience; measures his spent responsibilities and weighs his rôle's true worth that built up *toward* his highest aspiration for exalting *Truth,* as he saw it, that he may, judiciously, prescribe a pattern thereof:

"Full of wise saws and modern instances"

for those actors who follow.

The recapitulation of his accumulated resources, suitable for supervising "Life's" younger actors, reveals the acknowledged fact that he knows *about* many things foreign to his immediate activity, but that he only *knows* in a true sense, the cues to his elected "Life" rôle, which have been written in the ink of personal experience. He *knows* how to weave "Life's" threads of dreams, loves, and religion with the cords of ignorance, knowledge and temptation, mingled, good and ill together, into the tissue of his traditionally shaped rôle,—woven in pattern and color all his own. This knowledge of his experienced cues that crystallized his purpose in "Life,"

67

in the isolation of his being, proves only the "A B C"
knowledge of the grand drama being played by men
on the broad stage. The innumerable rôles in the
cast of men in the whole drama of "Life," from
the rising to the lowering of the World's curtain,
by the Omnipotent Manager, are to him, in all his
self-exalted wisdom, as the algebraic unknown quan-
tity!

Yet, Man labels the crystallization of his deter-
mined purpose in "Life," good or bad, "Success,"
though "no man knows. his *true* success," and im-
mediately assumes therefrom a self-laudable manner
that has been potent at terms in former ages. We
see the "Justice" of "Life,"

"With eyes severe"

in the egotism of his *power,* tempered, however, with
the precaution of experience. This life-thirst for
power, that invigorated his former activities and kept
"Life" from being stale, now, that it has been
quenched with the soothing liquid of efficiency, stimu-
lates a stern, deep satisfaction, a static rôle of semi-
independence from men. We see him in his hour
of efficient "Victory":—

> *"His tongue was framed to music*
> *And his hand was armed with skill,*
> *His face was the mould of beauty,*
> *And his heart the throne of will."*
> *—Emerson.*

68

His performance, that crowned his rôle with "distinction" may be that of an efficient hunter of the primitive era; a tiller of the soil; a body-servant; a tradesman in the market-place; a seaman; a manual laborer; a professional man, whatsoever focus for distinction he may have aimed, in his effort to sustain, produce and perpetuate the plot of "Life." To *achieve* was the goal.

Some men's achievement, in the eyes of the stage participants, appear more satisfactory than the achievement of fellow-men high on a neighboring "Mountain-top" of different range, their efficiency being made more conspicuous by the spot-light of the World's stage, shifted by the fickle public clamor being momentarily flashed upon them, and in the glare of this revealing light their accomplishments, apparently, supersede those of their fellow actors, who in surrounding shadow are participating with equal efficiency.

The measure of man's "Success" is for the Omnipotent Manager alone to determine, from the *motive* of man's works, which is secreted deep in the inner-soul of the actor. Whether or not his motive is in harmony with that of "Life's" plan, which grants him grace of soul peace with men and Manager.

> *"The bird that soars on highest wing*
> *Builds on the ground her lowly nest;*
> *And she that doth most sweetly sing,*
> *Sings in the shade where all things rest;*
> *In lark and nightingale we see*
> *What honor hath humility.*

"The saint that wears heaven's brightest crown
In deepest adoration bends;
The weight of glory bows him down
Then most, when most his soul ascends,
Nearest the throne itself must be
The footstool of humility."

Worldly actors may appraise their fellow-actors "Good" or "Bad," according to their point of view, their limited observation, their interpretation, their prejudice: be the actor a Monk, a Sailor, a "Crœsus," a "Dante," a "Rousseau," a Preacher, a Merchant or a Gypsy,—his *True Success* in "Life's" acting is accounted, only, by him and his Omnipotent Manager. We cannot see it, it makes no difference what havoc or clamor, what praise or censure his outward actions may have reaped from the on-looking world of actors.

The style of acting, arriving at the same climax, varies according to his position on the broad stage: he who achieves fame for efficiency among the tribes of the Dark Continents engages in a performance distinctly foreign to the rôle of the man in a more advanced civilization. The African on the Congo rug; the Hindu on the Indian rug; the Alaskan on the frozen northern fringe of the World's stage carpet, each in his traditional way, arrives at this Age of dignity. With all its limitations and with all its magnanimity, an age of *dignity,* it is. Man poised on the uppermost cube of the pyramid of immeasurable time! Of all past eternity that has been spent in nebular hypothesis, evolution, geology, —the "Justice" is the ripened fruit! Unreservedly,

70

to the "Justice," in all his goodness and all his badness, in all his wisdom and all his ignorance, in all his perfection and imperfection, Life's struggling actors, unitedly, bow in solemn homage to his acknowledged superiority in the art of "Life's" acting; he who has made his ins and outs; he who has learned his lessons (whether he follows them or not) ; he who knows the unbending general laws of "Life," against which he has ground his frictional way up "Life's" rocky road to the "Mountain-top."

"Faithful and friendly the arms that have helped me.
Cycles ferried and cradle, rowing and rowing like cheer-
    ful boatmen;
For room to me stars kept aside in their own rings;
They sent influences to look after what was to hold
    me. . . .

         .   .   .   .   .

All forces have been steadily employed to complete and
    delight me;
Now on this spot I stand with my robust soul."
                                    —Walt Whitman.

SCENE VI

SIXTH AGE

"Age shifts
Into the lean and slipper'd pantaloon,
With spectacles on nose and pouch on side,
His youthful hose, well saved, a world too wide
For his shrunk shank; and his big manly voice,
Turning again toward childish treble, pipes
And whistles in his sound."
—Shakespeare: "As You Like It."

PROGRAMME

TIME: Past, Present, Future.

CAST: "Age."

SCENE: A Mirage of "Life's" former Scenes, before *"THE RAINBOW ARCH."*

LIGHTING: Sunset.

ORCHESTRA: "Harmony" from Minor tones of Memory.

MANAGER: The Omnipotent.

Supporting the "Star of Life"

The Nazarene

73

SCENE VI

SIXTH AGE

"Age shifts
Into the lean and slipper'd pantaloon,
With spectacles on nose and pouch on side,
His youthful hose, well saved, a world too wide
For his shrunk shank; and his big manly voice,
Turning again toward childish treble, pipes
And whistles in his sound."
—Shakespeare: "As You Like It."

The real beauty of a picture is revealed by the last strokes of the artist's brush. So the Stage of "Life" is made most beautiful by the last touches Nature gives her picture as day declines, when with her lingering, loving caress, she kisses the fleeting, foamy clouds with sunshine's golden gleams, vivid, yet as delicate as morning's silver shafts, spraying the heavenly vault with a prismatic display of color, as if the Rainbow mist had been shattered for delicate heavenly adornment. The slipping "westering sun," that coquettishly plays hide and seek behind her feathery fan of mist, delights the sparkling lakes until they dimple in shifting shadow. After the frolic of the eve Nature's solemn love-light, in deepest hue, lingers delicately, in a tender mellow glow of golden calm over her painting of a day,—

75

her finished picture;—"Sublimity," throwing soft and silent rays on Man's, now, smooth earth-path that leads to *Peace.*

Yet, with far surpassing beauty, more delicate, intricate, infinite and wonderful; "Age," grand and profound, enters on Nature's stage of "Sublimity" to paint, with a master-hand, the last vivid strokes of "Life," giving subtle, delicate, veiled finishing strokes of an artist, obliterating and retouching, until we see the finished picture of "Harmony" in · act and spirit.

The stream of Time holds now, only the golden liquid of Life, the ills, the wearinesses, the uglinesses have been drunk, and are gone, "with the sorrows that are theirs," and only the beauty, the sweetness of "Life" are left in the stream for him to sup. We see him, all through "Age," drink sweet and beautiful memories from the river of Time, until the last molecule passes on with the current of Time into the ocean of Eternity,—back of the *Rainbow Arch!*

> *"Age,"* wrapped in his blanket of years,
> > "*Shifts*
> *Into the lean and slipper'd pantaloon,*
> *With spectacles on nose and pouch on side,*
> *His youthful hose, well saved, a world too wide*
> *For his shrunk shank; and his big manly voice,*
> *Turning again toward childish treble, pipes*
> *And whistles in his sound."*
> > *—Shakespeare: "As You Like It."*

Yet, beneath his shrunken, faded, wrinkled, threadbare temporal robe, that has been worn over the flowery paths of youth, the stormy fields of battle, the pinnacles of success, hides the perfect nurtured roots of *Youth's* sentiments, illusions and vagaries. Though the man be shriveled and warped, physically, by the snow of years, the distilled perfume of *Youth's* unfolded flowers is with him to sweeten "Age."

Minor tones of "Memory" play a melody, sweet in echoes of "Life's" former scenes, as glimmering mirages of his innocent Childhood, radiant Youth and stern Manhood, float in from the "Sands of Time," making "Age's" irradiant, retrospective scene one with poetic glamour. He—

> *"Stealest fire*
> *From the fountains of the past,*
> *To glorify the present."*
> *—Tennyson.*

As the glowing, beautiful scenes of "Life's" garnered harvest float vividly into realistic view through the misty glimmer of Memory's mirage, all despondency of Age's physical decrepitude vanishes and in illusion he lives without exertion, for

> *"To dream the old dreams over is a luxury divine"*

when truant fancy wanders to the old sweet scenes of time.

> *"Hardly we learn to wield the blade, before*
> *The wrist grows stiff and old;*
> *Hardly we learn to ply the pen, ere Thought*
> *And Fancy faint with cold."*
> *—Burton.*

77

> *"Last Age of all,*
> *That ends this strange eventful history,*
> *Is second childishness and mere oblivion."*

Yet, "Life is as long as each man has a 'Today' " this side of the *Rainbow Arch!*

In the tranquil evening glow of twilight, when the lips of night whisper messages of rest, and earth's sweet lilies inactively close their delicately frail petals in sweet repose, Man, too, in his physical fragility, closes involuntarily his withered, faded and failing presentative and representative petals:

> *"Sans teeth, sans eyes, sans taste."*

They sink in sleep, leaving Man richer and fuller in the power for which he used them during the Play of "Life"; the power to reason, to hope, to discern truth, to love, to think, to will; Man's soul-power, and in deep soul-communion, he dreams!

.   .   .   .

Man of men, a member of "Life's" acting company:

> *". . . The human race,*
> *Of every tongue, of every place,*
> *Caucasian, Coptic, or Malay,*

78

All that inhabit this great earth,
Whatever be their rank or worth."
—Longfellow.

has always acknowledged, since he became a responsible being, conscious of the *"Spark of Divinity"* within him, that he is allied to a superior power, an Omnipotent God and Manager, who has his highest reverence: a "Zeus," a "Jupiter," an "Allah," a "Jehovah," *God,*—named to suit his time and place. He interprets his part in "Life" according to his understanding of the Omnipotent's will, until his grand earthly *rehearsal* is finished for his true *Life eternal* rôle beyond the canopy of the *Rainbow Arch,* when he passes in peace, out of the stage-world's wing of time:

"Sans everything!"

Yet:

"Life is real! Life is earnest!
And the grave is not its goal;
'Dust thou art, to dust returnest,'
Was not spoken of the soul."
—Longfellow.

For the *Nazarene* left his rainbow-circled throne of light for wonderings sad and lone, in weariness and woe of earthly night: "God," the Omnipotent, manifest in the flesh of Man; the perfect, spotless, sinless *"Star of Life,"* who came, according to God's incarnation plan, to save and to redeem perplexed, distracted and lost Man for the emancipa-

79

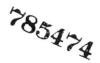

tion of "Life" eternal—back of the *Rainbow Arch,*
where:

"Eye hath not seen, nor ear heard,
 Neither have entered into the heart of man,
 The things which God hath prepared for them that love
  him."
—*I Corinthians, 2:9.*

"WHEN EARTH'S LAST PICTURE IS PAINTED"

(Back of the Rainbow arch!)

"When Earth's last picture is painted, and the tubes are
  twisted and dried,
When the oldest colors have faded, and the youngest
  critic has died,
We shall rest, and, faith, we shall need it—lie down for
  an aeon or two,
Till the master of all good workmen shall set us to work
  anew!

"And only the master shall praise us, and only the master
  shall blame;
And no one shall work for money, and no one shall
  work for fame;
But each for the joy of the working, and each, in his
  separate star,
Shall draw the Thing as he sees it for the God of Things
  as they Are!"

—*Rudyard Kipling.*